Contact: Allen or Brian for dynamic, high energy, life changing staff development!

Twitter: @Allenmendler

             @Brianmendler
             #30secpd

Facebook: facebook/TLCseminars (testimonials)

Phone: 800-772-5227

Email: Jon.Crabbe@tlc-sems.com

Teacher
Learning
Center

Printed in the United States of America

ISBN 978-0-9655115-3-7

Dedications

To my incredible family, wonderful friends and 'friends of Bill' for your sensitivity and support these last few years that have helped me to personally realize that virtually any problem can be overcome with determination, commitment, attitude and love.

Allen Mendler

To my childhood friend, Chris Fitzgerald. I think about you often. RIP.

Brian Mendler

Dr. Allen N. Mendler, provides seminars and consultation on topics related to teaching and reaching challenging students. He specializes in helping educators learn to motivate and handle difficult students, deal effectively with tough parents and provide effective school and classroom discipline. He is a school psychologist, parent, grandparent, teacher, educational consultant, and seminar leader based in Rochester, New York. As the internationally acclaimed co-author of *Discipline with Dignity*, Dr. Mendler has given thousands of workshops and is highly acclaimed as a motivational speaker and trainer. He was presented with the esteemed Crazy Horse Award for courage in reaching disadvantaged youth and recognized for his outstanding teaching by many organizations including the Bureau of Education and Research. Dr. Mendler is the author or co-author of numerous books including *When Teaching Gets Tough, The Resilient Teacher, Connecting with Students, and Motivating Students Who Don't Care*. His articles have appeared in many journals including *Educational Leadership* and he blogs for numerous sites for educators including *Edutopia* and *The Teacher Learning Center*.

Brian Mendler is one of the most sought after education speakers in America. His seminars are dynamic, high energy and thought provoking. Over the past nine years he has taught workshops to educators in America, Canada, England and Australia focusing on how to succeed with the most challenging students. His perspective is unique. It is not often you hear from an educator with severe ADHD that struggled in school himself. Brian pulls no punches. He tells it like it is without worrying about political correctness. His seminar will make you laugh, cry, and think about your most difficult students in an entirely new way. Brian makes very clear that building and then maintaining relationships is the single most important thing a teacher can do. He will help even the most reluctant educator to connect with any child. Mr. Mendler has authored numerous books on the topic. He co-authored the international best seller, *Discipline with Dignity 3rd edition*. His books *The Taming of the Crew and That One Kid* are also national best sellers. He has been interviewed by *USA Today* and regularly contributes to articles and news stories pertaining to this topic. Brian has worked as an adjunct instructor at St. John Fisher College in Rochester NY and volunteers with Special Olympics and Big Brothers Big Sisters. For daily updates, suggestions and strategies, join his many followers on social media. #30secpd. Brian lives with his wife, two young children and two pets.

Acknowledgements

We would like to thank the thousands of wonderful, talented, dedicated educators from every corner of the country and around the world who make a difference in the lives of our students. The many who have attended our workshops, seminars, school visits and training sessions deserve special appreciation since we have learned so much from you. It is the challenges you face daily to enrich the lives of your students that inspire us to create and adapt strategies that can hopefully lead to success for them and greater satisfaction for you. During the training sessions with educators on how to successfully work with difficult students, we have increasingly had teachers say, "It's not so much the kids that are the problem. It's the parents." While most parents are eager to cooperate with educators to secure what is best for their child, for a variety of reasons some resort to excuses, blame, accusations and anger when their child experiences difficulties and educators seek their support. This book provides strategies that apply to all parents with whom we interact, but will be especially helpful with those whose cooperation is often difficult to get.

In addition to the teachers, administrators and parents, a special thanks to Jon Crabbe, Elizabeth Sherwood and Dianne Long for their devotion and dedication to the Teacher Learning Center. Also a special thanks to Stefani Roth, Allison Scott and Ross Romano at ASCD, Claudia Wheatley and Jeff Jones at Solutions Tree.

Thanks to my wife Renee and our beautiful children Elijah and Brooklyn. You inspire me to be a better man every day. I love you.

Brian

The following Educators continue to positively impact the lives of our most challenging students and parents. Each of you inspires us to be better educators.

Tracy	Adams	LBD
Gregory R.	Annoni	Assistant Principal
Sandy	Austin	ELA Teacher – Retired
Michelle	Bahnsen	Behavior Coach
Debbie	Baldwin	Teacher – Retired
Nora	Ballwanz	EBD
Amanda	Barringer-Seigel	ELA Teacher – 4th grade
Brian	Benner	Physical Education Teacher
Debbie	Biastre	Director of Curriculum and Instruction
Jennifer	Blake	Dean of Students
Brian	Bode	Teacher – 5th grade
Janet	Boyd	Paraprofessional
Robert	Brice	Instructional Aide - Retired
Katie	Butcher	Teacher – 4th grade
Richard	Carnes	Assistant Principal
Jess	Davis	Teacher – 5th grade
Jackie	Davis, M.Ed	Director of Instruction
Bridget	DeMarse	Math & Technology Teacher
Debbie	Denmead Cassady	Speech/Language Pathologist
Johnny	Devillier	Biology Teacher
Dawn	Dickinson	Health Education Teacher
Mike	Dillman	Principal
Melanie M.	Ellenbecker, B.S., M.S.	EBD Special Education Teacher
Maura	Elliott	Teacher – 2nd grade
Amy	Ellison Culver	Teacher – Kindergarten
Laura	Espinoza-Nazzari	Teacher
Michele	Farley	Special Education Teacher
Melanie	Floyd	EBD Teacher
Noelle	Frederick	Self-Contained K-2 SPED Teacher
Liz	Grier	Middle School Special Education Support Teacher
Mollie	Guillory-Wagner	Special Education-Inclusion
Carolyn	Gutowski	Teacher
Stephanie	Haines	Special Education Teacher
Dr. Sarah R.	Hartman	Assistant Professor of Teacher Education
Angel	Hauert	Academy Coordinator
Stephen	Hickson	Teacher – 8th grade
Crystal	Hinkel	Teacher – 5th grade

Elizabeth	Ingrao	Alternative School Instructor
Debi	Jaeke	School Counselor
Desi	Johnson	ESL Teacher
Eric	Johnson	Teacher – 8th grade
Tim	Kelleher	Teacher
April	Kelly	7th grade Life Science Teacher
Sarah	Kelly	Teacher – 4th grade
Cindy	Kozel	Intervention Specialist
Brenda	Lane	Middle School Teacher
Stephanie	Levy	"2016 Georgia Teacher of the Year"
Adrienne	Mann	Teacher – 3rd grade
Pam	McDavid Sicca	School Counselor
Deirdre Denise	McKinley	Assistant Principal
Erica	Melly	Special Education Teacher
Jamie	Monaco	Special Education Teacher
Penny	Moses	Teacher – 2nd grade
Katie	Moss	School Psychologist
Christina	O'Hara	Stay-at-home wife/mother
Teresa	Quibell	Special Education Teacher
Kaitlin	Rando	English Teacher
Rachel	Reff	ESL Teacher
Diana	Riemenschneider	8th grade Math Teacher
Shannon	Robertson	Dean of Students
Catherine	Rosato	AIS Reading Teacher
Heidi	Scalf	Teacher – 4th grade
Chrystal	Schaffner	Special Education Teacher
Lauren	Shearing	Teacher – 1st grade
Lisa	Smith	Teacher – 5th grade
Brad	Staley	Principal
Tara	Surprenant	Behavior Strategist
Lisa	Thielen	EBD Teacher
Kyle	Thompson	Assistant Regional Superintendent
Laura	Tobia	Special Education Teacher
Jane	Van Alstyne	Resource Inclusion Teacher
Andrew	Wade	Dean of Students
Manny	Escobar	
Tim	Gorts	
Janie	Trevino	
Sharon	Zafiris	

Table of Contents

Chapter 1   Lay THE GROUNDWORK   11

Chapter 2   reasons PARENTS CAN BE DIFFICULT   13

Chapter 3   the BIG PICTURE   19

Chapter 4   SET THE RIGHT TONE with difficult parents   23

Chapter 5   KEY VALUES required for success   28

Chapter 6   Strategies to GAIN AND KEEP PARENTAL   31
             SUPPORT throughout the year

Chapter 7   EMPOWER difficult parents   37

Chapter 8   Strategies that PROVIDE SUPPORT &   44
             ADVICE for parents

Chapter 9   Strategies for HANDLING DIFFICULT   55
             MOMENTS with parents

Conclusion   64

Introduction

"Really! **We have no problems with him** *at home."*

*"***I don't understand why you are picking on my kid.*** But if it doesn't stop, you and I are going to have problems."*

"Why is my daughter always the one getting in trouble? **I feel like you have favorites!"**

*"***Frankie has never had a problem in school before.*** I'm not sure that his style of learning is best suited to your style of teaching."*

*"***Johnny just needs a little more individual attention*** and then I am sure everything will be fine."*

"How could you possibly have given her that grade?!?!"

"Billy is super smart. **I think the problem might be that he is not being sufficiently challenged."**

There is a cartoon by John McPherson in which a teacher introduces herself to her class and writes the following on the board: "don't like my teaching: call 1-800-you-fail." If only we could actually do that and not lose our jobs! Unfortunately, times have changed. It used to be that most teachers experienced a sense of autonomy and trust from parents. Rarely did we look over our shoulders for every decision. It was implied that the parent would support the teacher. Although most parents today are very supportive of teachers and feel good about their child's school, it has become more common for parents to blame the teacher when their child is having or creating problems. Rather than expecting their child to adapt, problems are attributed to the teacher's lack of sensitivity or poor teaching.

Parents in the lives of teachers are a mixed bag. By and large, they are a blessing. Virtually all of the data on student performance links high achievement and appropriate behavior at school to positive parent involvement in the education of their child. Of particular interest is that high achievement is associated more with parent-child communication at home than with parental involvement at school. All told, involved parents are crucial for student success. Many become and stay involved in very helpful ways, especially in an era of diminishing resources. In many schools, parent volunteers offer added supervision, mentoring and tutoring. Increasingly, strong PTAs conduct fundraisers to support extracurricular activities otherwise subject to budget cuts. Although most parents appreciate our efforts, very few truly understand the energy required to teach. Many parents are themselves overwhelmed by the stresses of life and have little patience for hearing about problems involving their children. Some center their lives around their children and feel a need to control every little detail. It is increasingly common for many to react with defensiveness and anger when we express our concerns, and they are quick to blame us when their children complain to them about a perceived teacher injustice. Many take complaints right to Administration, completely bypassing the teacher. Fortunately, the best administrators will insist upon the teacher's presence before fully listening to a parent's complaint with the exception of concerns involving accusations of abuse. Some parents may not understand or choose not to recognize that their child is one of many students in class and that our job is to teach all students. Worse, a fair number of difficult parents seem insensitive to the havoc caused by their child, which often results in others' inability to learn. Some parents are literally difficult to reach because of their absence and lack of involvement in their child's life. The bottom line is that parents have the power to be either a tremendous asset to us or a major misery maker. This book is about how to gain and keep the support of all parents, including those who are known to regularly blame, complain, and push our buttons.

Chapter One
Lay THE GROUNDWORK

Take time to tell parents exactly how your classroom will work. Make a list of all topics to discuss with them. You might begin by asking yourself what you'd like to know from a teacher to whom your child was assigned. Cover each briefly. Be sure to include the top two or three ways for students to be successful in your class. For example:

Dear Parent(s),

My name is Mr. Mendler and I am writing to welcome you and your child to my class this year. I am excited to let you know some of the more important procedures I use in our classroom to help each child be successful. Please discuss this letter with your child before school begins. Perhaps the most important thing to know about me is that I try every day to have each student experience success because I believe that is the most important way for students to get and stay motivated. Since there are differences in skills and work habits among students, I might give different tests, quizzes, homework assignments and consequences to different students. Some might get extended time or an opportunity to take a test more than once. Others may require special interventions to help them better concentrate or cooperate. My primary goal is to be fair to each student by giving each what s/he needs. If you ever have a question, concern or suggestion that can help me do my best for your child, please let me know. Please understand that I don't share details about why I might be doing something different with another student for reasons of privacy and respect.

Contacting Me: *I will be at my computer every Wednesday afternoon from 3pm-4pm. Barring an emergency or something unexpected, I will use that time to answer all emails received during the week at the latest.*

I will do my best to get back to you earlier if possible. If you communicate by email, I would appreciate receiving your email at least 24 hours in advance with an idea of what you would like to discuss. If you prefer to talk by phone, Thursday between 4-5 pm is best for me. Before contacting me, if there is a problem that you think requires my attention, please first talk with your child about coming to see me about it. Since a major goal in our class is developing responsibility, problems should be viewed as opportunities for our children to learn how to take care of themselves. Of course, please contact me immediately if the problem persists or if your child's safety seems at risk.

Late work / homework policy: *The expectation is for work to be handed in when it is due. If it is not on time, I need to understand why it is late. Sometimes points will be deducted. Other times they may not. Each situation will be handled individually. Since most assignments are primarily for your child to practice or use skills s/he already has, they should take no more than (ten minutes per grade level total). If there are extenuating circumstances or you notice your child stressed or struggling when doing homework, please let me know and we will work something out. My goal is for all kids to be successful in my class.*

Chapter Two

Reasons PARENTS CAN BE DIFFICULT

We haven't met a parent who upon experiencing the birth of their child starts planning how they will be as adversarial as possible when this child goes off to school. Nobody wonders, "Let me think of all the ways to be disagreeable so that I can dump on the teacher my kid gets in fifth grade!" Although most parents are cooperative and responsive, the first step towards working collaboratively with challenging parents is understanding and becoming sensitive to the likely factors in their lives and experiences that are usually at the core of their undesirable responses.

They see things differently. Some parents may not agree with the procedures and practices that you have established. It can be very frustrating when parents believe the teacher is doing things that they think fails to bring out the best in their child. From grading practices to seating arrangements, all teachers have to make hundreds of decisions each day and are therefore subject to all kinds of criticism. By telling parents ahead of time exactly how your room works you take the guessing away. I recall the annoyance I felt with my daughter's third grade teacher who had implemented a classroom color-coded behavioral system that enabled all students to earn rewards or lose privileges. While my daughter was usually a compliant child who often gained additional rewards for being cooperative, I did not think it was necessary for her to be rewarded for "good" behavior. She already knew that "good" behavior was expected, and using rewards to encourage more of what she could already do automatically, made little sense to me. As well, there is an abundance of research that shows how rewarding children for behaviors they have already mastered diminishes intrinsic motivation and leads to feelings of entitlement.

Although I chose not to challenge this practice (I mostly loved this teacher), it was my belief that the system did little to teach my daughter about responsibility. Although this teacher probably valued the importance of promoting responsibility in children, my guess is that her concerns about classroom management were more prominent and therefore guided her decision-making. Obviously, a parent's child is his only concern, whereas a teacher has to think about the needs of many students simultaneously. The different roles can easily lead to different perspectives and the valuing of different priorities. Although it is impossible to make all parents happy, the wise teacher looks for opportunities to invite parental input about classroom practices before problems arise. Remember, parents often know their children better than anyone else. Allow them to give input. Just be sure it is done in a structured, organized way.

They can't let go. Popularly known as "helicopter parents," these parents' actions are dominated by the need to constantly feel in control of all events that might have even the slightest chance of impacting their child. Sadly, they are driven by their unrelenting fear and anxiety, needing to be involved and in-charge of all aspects of their child's life. They volunteer for everything, show up at every classroom party and constantly email the teacher. They are a major time drain for teachers. A teacher we know had one parent email her 52 times during the first three weeks of school before they had a meeting to get this to stop. Although this led to a temporary reduction, the parent always acted like there was an emergency situation. In a few school districts, the problem of "helicopter" parents became so intense that they rate parents on a scale of 1 to 10 ("low maintenance" to "high maintenance") for purposes of equal distribution. One of the best ways to get this kind of excessive behavior to stop is to say, "*You are a very caring parent and your child is very fortunate to have you. I am sure that like all good parents, you want your child to grow up and make really good decisions. Although it may seem far away, Sal will one day become independent and will need to take care of himself. To help prepare children for that day, I try to teach them how to make good decisions when their parents are not present. So far, you* *have either called or emailed several times, trying to take care of one issue or another. Would you be willing to tell Sal to see me first before you contact me? Of course, let me know if the problem persists. It is rare for me to hear from parents more than once or twice because usually we are able to take care of it in class. I'll contact you if there's a problem that we can't solve and if you'd like, I would be happy to send you a feedback note (phone call; email) at the end of the week. Are you okay with that?*

Rightly or wrongly, they believe the teacher does not care about their child. The reality is some students are harder to like than others. Difficult students often go out of their way to make themselves appear as behaviorally unattractive and unappealing as possible. Making matters worse is that these students always seem present. Students are most often difficult when one or more of their basic life needs is not being fulfilled. In an effort to feel more connected to others, it is common for some to do a lot of irritating things to get noticed. When they believe they will be unsuccessful, some act out or become unmotivated. Others may lack self-control, become disruptive within the classroom and therefore difficult to like. Some may purposely provoke the teacher so that the teacher will act mean and unfair. The student may then go home and tell her parent(s) just how mean and unfair the teacher is.

As an adult, it requires a great deal of professionalism to set aside personal likes and dislikes. I recently taught a seminar at a private school outside of Baltimore. Before introducing me, the principal asked for teachers to share good news with the group. A sixth grade teacher raised her hand and said, "Apparently Damian either moved or is somewhere else because I just found out that thankfully he is not coming back next year!" The 7th grade teachers let out a raucous applause, obviously thrilled at this news. This struck me as the equivalent of a group of doctors delighted at the news of a patient with a particularly resistant disease leaving the hospital with no knowledge of his whereabouts. To celebrate a student leaving without any idea where he is going is a disservice to our community and the profession. While we may need to occasionally advocate for an alternative placement that can better benefit a student, the foundation of success with challenging kids is the refusal to give up on them.

We must believe we can succeed with any child put in front of us. It is each educator's obligation to attempt to reach and give our all to motivate every child despite personal preferences. We must also force ourselves to remember that professionalism calls for the respectful and dignified treatment of all students and their parents, including those who may be as irritating and obnoxious as their child.

They disliked school and may harbor resentment. Many students who struggle in school have parents that experienced similar struggles. Like their child, these parents often had a school experience that was connected to feelings of failure and/or discomfort. As a result, they are often on-guard and defensive to the basic sights, sounds and smells of school. When their children struggle, they can quickly become angry and defensive. They are usually hyper-vigilant to perceived injustice and discrimination, and quick to blame or attack. When their phone rings during the day, waves of dread anticipating bad school news are common. Dread rapidly turns to anger when their fears are confirmed. Since a successful school experience is so dependent upon positive parent support, the challenge is to help these parents create a different picture of school from the one they expect. While conducting training we sometimes ask parents and teachers to remember a time at school when they started out feeling negative but wound up feeling positive. Maybe you initially thought the teacher was mean or the subject was too hard. Maybe you felt uncomfortable around the other kids. Maybe you lacked confidence at first. Maybe it was something else entirely. It can help to think of a subject that you started out hating when you were at school, but wound up loving. What specifically turned things around? How did the teacher help change your attitude? The goal is to bring behaviors like these to your interactions with students and their parents on a regular basis so that they can begin to get a different picture of what school can be.

They are struggling to raise their children in a complex world and are having limited success. There are a myriad of influences that affect our youth including the bombardment of social media sites that allow kids to literally escape into a virtual world, video games, easy availability of drugs and alcohol, gangs, and on and on. As professionals, we know these issues well, but on a personal level, these create never-ending struggles and challenges for all of us. I marvel at how much time my daughter spent each morning checking and re-checking to make sure that not a hair was out of place before school. Although she found ways of doing well at school, I often wondered how much better she could have done if she had spent more time reading and less time texting or instant messaging. For parents, it takes a lot of time, energy, love and limit-setting to maintain influence. A combination of child temperament and parental frustration can reduce the impact of parents on shaping their child's behavior. For example, some parents get to a point of utter exasperation with their child who refuses to do homework or value school sufficiently to care about getting good grades. Rather than constantly battling, some eventually back off in an effort to preserve a positive relationship. When educators contact them about a school concern, the feeling of helplessness is often expressed as frustration and anger towards us.

Children can be utterly determined to press and nag parents for what they want. One informal survey of teenagers found that when they crave something new, most expect to ask nine times before parents give in. Educators need to express our understanding of the difficulties parents are likely facing so that we can form an alliance to help their child by learning how to set and enforce limits. An idea for this is to start every phone call home with something positive: "Your daughter is one of the most determined young women I know. When she believes something she fights like crazy. I really like this about her." It is always possible to find at least one nice thing to say about any student even when there are concerns and we are seeking assistance. Our suggestions are more likely to be greeted with appreciation and cooperation when parents sense that teachers understand the challenges they face. For example, "Because she is so determined, I sometimes find that she easily gets upset when she thinks others are telling her what to do and when she is upset, it can be hard to calm her down at school. Do you see that at home? Have you noticed anything that can be especially helpful in those situations?"

They do not or cannot value the importance of school. Many
parents who have good intentions and value the importance of a
good education for their children are unable to provide the necessary
stability because some are literally trying to make ends meet. If a
family must move several times during a school year and the child is
bounced between schools, it is almost impossible to succeed. Although education may be valued, the reality of providing for more
basic needs often takes precedent. We recently worked at a school in
a rural area outside Des Moines where 60% of the high school kids
work 6-8 hours each day on the family farm. While most work before
and after school, there can be little time, energy and enthusiasm left
for homework. Because of these realities, reaching challenging parents often requires considerable work in the communities we teach.
An inner city school in Washington DC has a family barbecue the
weekend before school begins. Parents are shown a brief video of
school expectations before everyone eats together. We must become
sensitized to the social and cultural community values while preach-
ing the importance of making academics the number one priority in
every young person's life.

***They are angry people and school is one more place to express
their misery***. Some people always seem miserable while others are
always optimistic. Most are somewhere in-between. The best teachers
build relationships with parents the same way they do with kids. They
get to know likes and dislikes. They ask about their work life. If a
parent works multiple jobs just to keep food on the table, a quick positive call or text about their child and a thank you for their hard work
means so much. Remember that the child of an unhappy parent is
likely to need more compassion from his or her teacher. Many difficult parents were poorly parented and carry unresolved resentment
towards those in authority. At the same time, try not to back down
on policies and procedures that are educationally sound but may be
targeted as a bulls-eye for a parent's anger. Chapter nine shows how
to best defuse angry parents when they don't get their way.

Chapter Three
The BIG PICTURE

There are five beneficial ways to view challenging parents that are at the core of all strategies offered in this book. Embracing these makes it much easier to work effectively with them.

View difficult parents as misguided advocates. How we perceive people strongly influences our behavior towards them. For example, a person who doesn't easily cooperate and follow rules can be viewed as "oppositional" or "independent-minded." A child who won't take "no" for an answer could be seen as "annoying" or "strong-willed." We believe that an angry parent is usually better than an absent parent! While angry parents can be unpleasant and sometimes inappropriate, their anger conveys advocacy for their child. When we view complaints, anger and accusations as misguided advocacy, it makes it possible for us to continue working with the parent because the only issue is our disagreement with what is being advocated and/or how it is being expressed. Virtually all parents, including most that act irrationally, will cooperate if they really believe that you care about their child achieving success and are helping their child become more responsible. We recall an angry parent calling to complain about the amount of homework I gave her son. She said, "It is ridiculous that my son is spending two hours on his math homework." My response: "I had no idea it would take him two hours. You are right and I am sorry. That was not my goal. Thanks for letting me know. In the future I'll try to give him a more appropriate assignment that shouldn't take more than about thirty minutes. I'll let him know to see me if it ever does. Sound good?" If you make a mistake there is nothing better than saying you are sorry.

View difficult parents as having something to teach. When parents feel appreciated, their cooperation almost always improves. Be open to parent suggestions, ideas, and dialogue about how you can help their child become more successful and/or responsible. Acknowledge your limitations and seek their support (i.e. "If you have any other ideas about how I can help your child, please let me know what they are." Or, "Can you tell me how you get him to cooperate at home when he has a mind of his own?"). Behaving this way often defuses a parent's anger and opens the door to mutual problem solving. Push to get beyond raw emotions and see things from the parent's perspective.

We remember Mrs. Stevens, whose presence and complaints made teachers of Danny, her physically disabled and learning impaired son, roll their eyes upon seeing her. She was ornery, sarcastic and caustic. She seemed to focus on the negative despite many fine efforts being made to accommodate her son by school professionals. In short, a visit from Mrs. Stevens was an unpleasant event. In actuality, her frustration was often palpable as she struggled to get a supportive but rigid school system to address her child's needs. We came to respect Mrs. Stevens for her unyielding devotion to Danny. Once we got past her abrasive manner, we were able to learn a lot about Danny from listening to her. We were then able to develop many different learning strategies that not only helped Danny, but were also helpful to other students. Years later, she still expresses much caring and warmth to the educators who validated and embraced her ideas during that difficult time.

Reach out to difficult parents before you act. Parents who are chronically difficult usually have a need to feel power and influence. Most feel that nobody listens or really cares what they think. In fact, it is not unusual for them to believe (sometimes correctly) that they have lost much of their influence with their own children. Getting angry and blaming the school can be a way for them to form an alliance with their children against a common "enemy." It can be very effective to seek opinions from these parents before they complain. Invite them to come to school meetings when you know policy issues will be discussed so they can have input. When seeking parental input about classroom rules or procedures, parents who complain can actually be quite helpful. The idea is to give them a voice before complaining so they feel heard and respected. Opinions about how their child might react to something you are planning can be solicited as well. For example, after the usual greetings, you might say to a difficult parent, "My goal is for each student in the class to learn more about responsibility at the playground. Do you have ideas that you think could be good for your child and perhaps other children as well?"

Always let what is best for kids guide you. Do what is educationally sound and make your ultimate goal to improve student lives. Unfortunately, some educators and parents are more focused on doing what is best or easiest for them. If you base your decisions on what is best for each student, your actions may not always be appreciated but you will always be respected and usually applauded. Teachers need to be ready to explain the purpose of actions they take in terms of how these actions are designed to *teach the student responsibility or help the student achieve academic success.* Administrators need to consult teachers about intended actions before these actions are put into effect. Although not all conflict between a teacher and administrator generated by a complaining parent can be avoided, much of it can. Many educators are easily intimidated, believing they will receive little administrative support if parents complain. While it is true that few educators look forward to battling difficult parents, try hard not to allow your actions to be guided by fear. Perhaps of greatest importance for educators is that we give all of our students what we believe they need without worrying about treating each one the same way. If parents complain about unfair treatment that their child has received, we must be prepared to learn from the parent without backing away from doing what is best for every individual child. As Thomas Jefferson said long ago, "there is nothing so unequal as treating unequals equally."

***Stay in control of yourself and maintain your dignity at all
times***. It is easy to act with respect and dignity when all is going
well. The challenge is to convey these attitudes when anger, disagreement, and finger pointing come your way. Act like the best professional athletes who are great at remaining calm when everything around
them is chaotic. When needing to give feedback to a parent and you
are unsure what to say, put yourself at the receiving end. How would
you want to be spoken to by someone else who is about to give you
feedback about your child? If a parent gets mad and starts using language that you find offensive, act in a way that is consistent with what
you are trying to teach your students. What would you want your students to say or do if they were being verbally assaulted? How should
they react? If parents express anger, work to defuse them in a manner
similar to how you would want your students to defuse each other.

Be quick to forgive and difficult to offend. When working to get
the best out of people, it is fine to hold them accountable for their
actions, but be quick to forgive. Don't clutter your hard drive with
grudges when others say or do hurtful things. Mental toughness
means we always stay focused on our goals and what we are there to
accomplish. It is literally the most important component to being a
great teacher. Stay mentally strong at all times! Grudges do nothing
but waste our limited supply of energy. Smile, forgive, and move on.

Chapter Four
SET THE RIGHT TONE *with difficult parents*

Picture a difficult parent as a grizzly bear or mother lion protecting her cub. Perhaps the cub needs no protection because nobody means to do it harm, but does the mother know this? More than likely, she errs on the side of caution and scares off or possibly attacks even harmless intruders. Being a parent often feels like walking a tightrope of confusion while trying to figure out when to support and when to let go. Most difficult parents have come to view school as a threat to themselves or more likely their child. They must first trust that you are on their side before they welcome you into their den, and that requires finding as many ways as possible to let them know that their child's presence and success is as important to you as it is to them.

Get on their side early. In addition to what we wrote earlier about explaining exactly how your classroom is going to work, spend time going out of your way to build relationships with parents. Show that you care by enthusiastically expressing a desire to make it a successful year for their child. Parents give us slack when they believe we care about their child. Reported in the bestseller *BLINK* (2005), is a study conducted by Wendy Levinson. Hundreds of conversations between physicians and their patients were recorded. Roughly half of the doctors had been sued for malpractice at least twice with the other half never having been sued. Results found that there was no difference in the quantity or severity of medical mistakes between those who had been sued and those who had not. Physicians who had never been sued spent twenty percent more time with their patients and showed more personal interest by engaging in active listening. The bottom line is patients don't sue doctors they like who show they care. If physicians can avoid malpractice lawsuits by spending a few more caring minutes with a patient, it is reasonable to assume that teachers can benefit from this as well.

Have students call their parents. In most cases that require contacting a parent to discuss inappropriate behavior, it is most powerful and memorable to have the student make the call. The teacher should be present when the student calls her parent at home or at work. Ideally, the conversation should occur via speakerphone so that you can hear and when necessary participate in the proceedings. Younger children may lack the necessary sophistication of language, so we can provide cues, prompts and even scripts. Clyde Hill Elementary School in the Seattle area created a script *(figure 1)* that children can follow when parental contact is needed. A few adaptations have been included. Be sure to interject positive comments about the student during the phone call. If you know a student is physically or verbally abused please seek administrative and counselor advice before calling. It is never ok to knowingly put a child in harms way at home, no matter what they do in school.

CLYDE ELEMENTARY SCHOOL STUDENT SCRIPT FOR TELEPHONE CALL TO PARENT

Hello (Mom or Dad), this is (student's name).
I was asked to call you because I_____
_____. Mrs. _____(teacher) is sitting next to me right now and is listening to our conversation. What I did is against the rules and I was asked to talk with you about my decision to do this. The thing that I did wrong was_____.
The reason it is wrong is_____.
I learned_____. Next time I will_____. I will talk more with you about this when I get home, and I will make a better effort today to follow the school rules. Is there anything you want to say to my teacher or me before I say good-bye?

Figure 1

Have parents fill out an interest inventory. Learn the strengths and needs of your students as perceived by their parent(s). You can send and Interest Inventory *(figure 2)* home to all parents and request that they fill it out. A nice personalized cover letter explaining the purpose should accompany the inventory sheet. If you know in advance who your challenging students and/or parents might be, it is usually more effective to call them and use the inventory to elicit information from them. You might say something like, "To help each child be successful, I'd like to know a little about your child's interests and needs. I'll be sending a form home to all parents, but sometimes I like to call parents to ask. Can you tell me a little about what your child likes and doesn't like?"

INTEREST INVENTORY

Dear Parent:

My goal is to get to know your child! Please take a moment to fill out this interest inventory. I am eager to do whatever I can to make your child's school experience successful, meaningful and pleasant. I appreciate the opportunity to gain from your knowledge of your child. All information is kept completely confidential. Thank you.

My child's name / nickname is _____.

Something my child likes to do outside of school is_____.

My child's favorite time of year is_____.

For my child, school is_____.

When my child gets older, I hope_____.

During my child's free time, he/she prefers_____.

A place my child likes to visit is_____.

My child's favorite hobby is_____.

My child's favorite subject is school is_____.

With other people my child_____.

When my child does not get his/her way at home_____.

When my child is alone_____.

When my child misbehaves it works best to_____.

Important things to know about my child's life outside of school that might affect his/her achievement in the classroom are_____.

The single most important thing to know about my child is_____.

My child's greatest strength is_____.

My child's biggest weakness is_____.

Figure 2

A helpful quick quiz. If the fill-in sentences above do not work for you make up your own interest inventory or try our four-question quiz for parents.

Questions one and two: What are two qualities your child's favorite teacher had that you really liked?

1.

2.

Questions three and four: What are two qualities your child's least favorite teacher had that you really disliked?

3.

4.

This same quiz can be modified and given from teacher to student during the school year: What are the two best qualities about me as a teacher? If you were able to press a button on me and change any two things, what would they be and why?

Update your website. At a district, school or classroom level, develop and maintain a website that includes district/school/classroom news, resources and contact information as well as personalized information for each child. That could include students' real-time attendance and grades, assignments they did or did not complete, contact information for teachers and any other tracking information deemed appropriate. Requiring a bit more complexity, but entirely possible, it can also be the place for an interest inventory and other information that can be helpful to know from parents.

Consider using apps to stay in contact and eliminate language barriers. There are apps available that offer a safe, classroom-friendly communication tool to help teachers send messages to individual or groups of students and parents. Using the tool, teachers can send messages to students and families without disclosing personal contact information and without students and families having to share theirs. Some apps can translate the messages into as many as 70 languages, which is very useful for students who have non-English speaking parents. Ever have a call home escalate due to a parent not understanding what you are saying? Parents can communicate back and forth with the teacher and their child in their native language and every conversation is documented and kept in a digital file.

Consider a home visit. A home visit or a visit on neutral turf can be a very powerful way to develop a helpful rapport with parents. If the parent(s) seem uncomfortable having you in their home, meet at a neutral place for a cup of coffee. You should go with another teacher or support person. Sacramento City Schools train teachers who are interested, and suggests that everyone begin by explaining his or her relationship to the student. The goal is for educator and parent to share hopes and dreams for their child, share classroom expectations that lead to success and learn from the parent how s/he thinks you can help the child be successful. You want to primarily use this time to build a relationship. Try not to write things down as this may make the parent feel uncomfortable. If you can't do this with all parents, be sure to include at least some students who are doing well to avoid stigmatizing only the kids in trouble. Expect most meetings to last between thirty and forty-five minutes.

Chapter Five
KEY VALUES *required for success*

It is wise to inform parents about the values that will be the foundation of the classroom expectations (rules). These values should be based on what we know we need for good teaching and learning to occur. For example, you might say to parents, *"The most important values in my room are respect, responsibility, and safety. The way I like to express these to students is:* **take care of yourself; take care of each other; take care of this place**. *Based on each of these I have some specific expectations (rules) designed to instill these values. The expectation is everyone will keep hands and feet to themselves at all times. I am firm about this because respecting personal space is critical to a safe and respectful school year. I will also be asking our children to tell their expectations of respect."* Notice how the expectation is specific and measurable. If a parent questions your actions, tie them to a value (i.e. "I know that sometimes they're just pretending to fight like friends do, but when I ask them to stop it's about learning to respect personal space."). That is my focus. Based on the *value of responsibility* everyone will bring a notebook and pen to school every day. Notice the expectation is specific and tells the student exactly *what* to do. The *value* tells *why* the expectation is important. You might invite parents to offer their input about rules or procedures that they believe will best help their child behave in accordance with the values, especially if they are argumentative.

Involve students in developing expectations and let parents know. Students experience ownership when they have a voice in developing expectations. As a result, their involvement makes them more apt to follow them. And if they don't, parents are more likely to back away from complaining when they realize that their child participated in their development. For example, *"Ms. Jones, I'm not sure*

*if you realize this, but the students agreed that (name the expectation) is import-
ant. Luis was among them, so I think you might want to talk to him about why
he broke a rule that he agreed was important."* Explain to students how
values give expectations their foundation and meaning. While rules
are designed to tell students what to do or how to do it, the goal of a
value is defining why the specific expectations are needed. Without
values, expectations can feel arbitrary. With values, they make sense.
For example, a speed limit sign tells a driver how fast he may go (the
expectation), but is most likely to be followed in the absence of a po-
lice officer when it makes sense (the value). We are more apt to follow
a speed limit sign to slow down on a residential street in the middle
of the day when children are playing than we are at midnight on the
same street. Be sure that expectations apply to you (the teacher) as
well. For example, based on the value of student learning, tests will be
graded and returned within 48 hours.

**Seek administrative support by having values and expecta-
tions endorsed by them.** Explain why the values that you plan to
share are necessary for good teaching and learning to occur, and how
the expectations support the values. This is also a good time to let
your administrator know how you plan to involve parents and communicate with them. Let them know that if ever a dissatisfied parent
goes directly to them without first having spoken to you, you would
greatly appreciate them redirecting that parent your way before
taking action. As well, if you want input into administrative decisions
that are likely to impact a student's performance or behavior in your
class, this is a good time to ask to be involved before decisions are
finalized.

Don't gossip to parents or students about others. If a parent or
student questions your actions toward another student, avoid getting
into specifics. As indicated earlier, explain that you consider whatever
happened with the other student to be a private matter between yourself, the other student and her family. Acknowledge that you often do
different things with different students because you want to help each
become **successful** or learn more about **responsibility**.

You are at liberty only to say that if you did something different with another student it was because of these reasons. Let the parent know that you will also never talk about their child to another parent. Then turn the focus back on the person who is complaining. For example, "My belief is that this is the best consequence (test, quiz, homework assignment) for your child. Can you think of any better ways to help your child improve?

Agree to change any rule or consequence as long as an acceptable alternative is proposed. Whenever a parent or student complains about a rule or consequence that you believe is necessary, agree to change the rule as long as they propose an alternative that is acceptable to you. The alternative must have a high likelihood of promoting responsibility and facilitating success while maintaining order and keeping the classroom safe. It is unwise to argue with parents or students about specific rules and consequences. Stay focused on values: success, responsibility, order and safety. Your message needs to be, "Whenever there are problems in following rules, students are welcome to do _____ just as soon as they do_____."

Do not waver when it comes to goals and values, but be flexible in considering other ways in which those goals can be achieved. Sometimes we as teachers get so caught up with the homework or consequence that we forget what we want to accomplish with it. Homework, tests, quizzes, and consequences should be viewed as nothing more than vehicles to the destination. The destination is not negotiable. The student will stop calling others names or will show they know how to multiply. Does it really matter how many problems a student does to show us the skill is mastered? Negotiate the vehicle. Try to stay firm on the destination.

Chapter Six

Strategies to GAIN AND KEEP PARENTAL SUPPORT *throughout the year*

The strategies in this section have two goals. Some are designed to show ways of preventing problems from developing with difficult parents. These are simple, easy to implement strategies to make and keep your classroom a welcoming place. Other strategies show how to keep problems with difficult parents from dominating your time and energy.

Make the classroom a warm and friendly place. Although there are many factors that affect our students over which we have little control, we are in charge of the attitude that we bring to school every day. Most schools are filled with caring, compassionate adults dedicated to making school a great place. Be one of them. The saying "attitude is everything" applies mightily to the degree of success teachers experience. Strive to make your classroom become a retreat, an island or sanctuary of safety, support and connectedness to which students (and parents) look forward to coming. Students are our customers and content is our product. The goal is to get students and their parents to buy what we are selling. Think of a store or place you love to go. What characteristics of the people or environment make you want to go there? Is there music playing? What is the lighting like? What colors are on the walls? Are you greeted upon entering? Does anyone thank you for coming? Try to simulate these characteristics in your classroom in order to provide the equivalent of an attractive place. Gaining cooperation from difficult parents becomes much easier when their kids want to come to school and their parents feel welcome when they visit. Too often, we make parents feel like outsiders, welcoming them only during open school night in which they get to meet us in a very scripted, impersonal way. School signs should be friendly. Instead of "All visitors must report to the office," signs ought to state, *"If you are a parent, thank you for coming today. For safety reasons, please stop by the office to say hello and sign in."* A nice touch is to offer coffee and water in the office.

Offer feedback that inspires hope. The best way to avoid conflict with parents is to have satisfied students. Students tend to be most motivated and best behaved when the classroom is a relevant place, provides adequate depth and continually provides students with confidence and belief in their ability to be successful. Honest feedback that points to improvement is essential as well, but even corrective feedback is best received on a foundation of hope. The following are examples of oral or written feedback that tend to inspire hope in students. Make parents aware of adaptations they might use to motivate their child:

*"**Thanks for all the thought** you put into this assignment."*

*"It looks like **you really put forth some effort** on this."*

*"**I am especially impressed by** these ideas (specify)."*

*"**I like how** you_____.*

"It would be nice to read (hear) even more from you about _____."

*"Your answers show that **you are putting out some serious effort**. Keep it going!"*

*"**A good student like you** can show even more of the same ideas. Please give me two more examples."*

*"**You are well on your way** to..."*

*"**Your comments in class tell me that you know this content even better than you wrote.** All you need to do is write a few sentences*

just like you talk. See me after class and we will work on how to write your excellent thought even better."

"Your answers show that you are really getting there. *A little more on (specify) would make it even better. Keep it up!"*

The comments above emphasize *effort* more than *achievement*. Achievement is most likely to occur when students believe that *how* they do is directly linked to the amount of *effort* they give. Be sure to share these comments as privately as possible. If positive comments are offered publicly, some kids become concerned about losing the respect of their peers.

Emphasize your desire to promote success in their child.
Keep your focus on promoting success. Let the parent know what is expected for success to occur. Show flexibility in doing whatever it takes to help their child be successful but connect every suggestion parents have to this outcome. If they want you to do something that flies in the face of success, be honest. Tell them, *"Much as I would like to agree with you, I just can't do what you are asking. If I raised his grade I am afraid that I would be expecting less from your child than I know he is capable of achieving. Help me figure out what we can do that will help us all feel better and also help Bobby get his work done at a level we all know he is capable of."*
Parents respect teachers who have realistically high expectations of their child.

Text or email a positive message. A quick message to share appreciation about something positive done or accomplished by the student can be very powerful. We like texting because it is easy, can be done immediately when you want, there is a definitive record of the exchange, and according to a Dynmark report, 98% of text messages are read with 90 percent being read within 3 seconds. Compare that to email open rates of 20-30% and you see the power of sending a text message. Also, some parents might not have access to the internet, but almost everyone has a cell phone. In fact, you might want to show the student or read the text you are about to send to the student's parent(s) and ask for an okay before you send it. Keep your phone handy since you might want to take a photo of the child engaged in a meaningful activity and send it along with the message. Virtually all students will feel especially good having been noticed as well as knowing they have the remainder of the day to savor the positive interaction most are likely to have with their parent(s) when they go home. Be sure to check with your specific district for texting and picture policies.

When you give feedback to parents start with the positive. Even when meeting to discuss concerns and issues that need improvement, start with strengths. "Hi Mrs. Jones. I would like to start by asking you to tell me about Jennifer's strengths and I would like to share some things that I notice as well." Writing them down is an awesome visual and will immediately set the parent at ease during a potentially tense moment.

Jennifer's Strengths

Always is smiling

Stands up for herself

Has a mind of her own

Works hard when interested

Can be helpful towards others

Is a leader

Send complimentary notes home occasionally. Everyone likes to hear good news and will be much more receptive to cooperating when their help is needed. Make an effort at least twice a month in some form to make contact with the parent(s) of your challenging students. It can be very powerful to write a note to a parent of a poorly behaving student that had recently behaved well.

Dear Mrs. Smith,

I am writing to let you know that your son had a fantastic day. He has been really making an effort to pay more attention and get his work done. I am so proud of him. Please be sure to tell him how pleased you are and remind him to keep up the good work.

Another option is to show the same or similar note to a student who has been making an effort to improve. On a day when the behavior has taken a turn for the worse, ask him/her to let you know when s/he believes the time is right to send it home. Some teachers believe this will reinforce bad behavior. Although an understandable concern, remember that behavior change is a roller coaster ride filled with ups, downs, twists, turns and loops. Most students will see / hear the more powerful message of the teacher appreciation for behavioral improvement. Improved behavior usually follows because the student has been powerfully and privately thanked while reminded that s/he is entirely capable of offering better behavior.

Put the responsibility on your students for choices they may later regret. It gets tiring to hear about how missing homework assignments are due to the teacher's negligence or how a poor grade on the test is due to the teacher not having taught the material properly. Landing in the office for disciplinary action must be the result of a "set-up" by either the teacher or another student! Many of these blaming complaints can be easily prevented. For example, when students do not do their homework, have them write the excuse on an index card. Put the dated cards in the student's portfolio so that it is available at the next parent-teacher conference. If you give students opportunities to improve their grades by either staying after school for extra help, revising the assignment or re-taking the test (and they do none of the above), ask them to write a sentence or two acknowledging their choice (i.e. "Mrs. Hahn gave me three opportunities to improve my grade on the test, and I decided against doing any of them."). Be sure that the statement is dated and then placed in the student's file. Ultimately the goal is to teach powerful lessons about responsibility while reducing parental excusing and enabling.

Take complaints seriously. Like the boy who cried 'wolf', it is not unusual to psychologically dismiss parents who regularly complain especially if they or their children are hard to like. Ms. Langdon was such a parent. I remember working with her son Dylan who regularly did little irritating things sneakily to his classmates and would then complain that he was being bullied. His mother would angrily call the school wondering why nothing was being done to the other kids while he was often getting into trouble. Obviously, Dylan was going home and telling Mom that he was being unfairly picked on. While listening carefully to her concerns one day, she named three students with solid positive reputations who she claimed had been extorting money from Dylan by threatening to beat him up. The boys persisted for a while in denying these accusations. If not for the greater persistence by the vigilant Assistant Principal who eventually got the boys to admit their involvement, the incident could have been swept under the rug since most school people were fed up with both Dylan and his mother. If there are constant complaints, there may be some truth so it is important to take all complaints seriously.

Refer to their child as "our child." Whenever speaking to a parent, talk about "our" child. For example, Ms. Jones calls with concerns about Jamie's low achievement in your class. Listen to her concerns. When the time comes for problem solving, ask, "What do you think we can do to help Jamie succeed? I look forward to helping our young man any way I can."

Chapter Seven

EMPOWER *difficult parents*

The goal of this chapter is to help you think of as many ways as possible to make parents feel important at school. For example, ask parents to record children's books or textbook material for the school's audio book library. Seek difficult parents to help guide follow-up to lessons with individual students or small groups. Get them and their kids involved in school beautification projects. We know of a school outside Boston that has a "grounds committee" made up of multiple parents. Monthly, they and their kids meet at school to make sure there is no trash on building grounds. During the spring, they plant and nourish vegetables on school property. When grown, they take half for themselves and give half to a food shelter. Invite challenging parents or parents of challenging students to sit on advisory or decision-making school committees that have parent representation on such topics as improving school climate and developing after-school activities. Seek their involvement in selecting respected community speakers to talk to kids and/or parents on relevant topics of concern like drug use/abuse, overcoming the impact of poverty, alternatives to violence etc. Perhaps the easiest way to empower parents is to simply ask them questions, seek information, or ask their opinion about their child and then be a good listener.

Consider the impact of assignments and projects on parents.
Assignments and projects should be given with the expectation that at most minimal parental involvement will be required. We believe school assignments should be the teacher's responsibility to provide whatever materials and organizational support necessary with minimal academic help coming from home. Give as much specific information as you can to parents about assignments that do require their help.

Try to give assignments that require no more than ten minutes total per grade level through middle school and no more than ten to fifteen minutes total per grade level through high school. Much research has shown that exceeding these limits is usually counter-productive. If parents notice that their child becomes easily frustrated or is regularly exceeding these guidelines, tell them to let you know. This can be spelled out when you lay the groundwork, but will likely need to be reinforced with some students and their parents. Assignments that motivate tap into existing skills or interests so stay away from assigning homework that requires learning new concepts. If you know in advance that some or many of your students will need academic or logistical help from their parents, let parents know in advance and try hard to make the project enjoyable. If you want or expect parents to guide or check a project, give them rubrics so they know what to look for in their child's work. For projects where students often need to meet with peers outside of school, be sensitive to geographic groupings. If you know a few students live on the same street do your best to group them together for these projects. Minimize the need to shop for supplies. Some families have limited access to transportation. If parents will have to shop for materials with their children, explain specifics and provide organizational support. Although it is reasonable to expect some academic help from home, there are some students in each school whose parents are physically, intellectually, or emotionally unavailable to provide the level of support needed for success. In some cases, there is simply too much of this requirement hoisted upon parents. Students should not be punished for parents who cannot or will not provide the type of support that might be needed.

Have a suggestion box. Welcome input from your students and their parents by having a suggestion box. If parents do not want to contact you directly, their child can bring suggestions from home and drop them in the box. This can be done anonymously if a parent prefers. Remember to keep an open mind. Let all know that you read them daily, and if signed, you will contact the parent for more discussion.

Make parent conferences inviting. Unfortunately, for a variety of reasons, some schools get very low turnout on parent conference nights. One way to facilitate better attendance is by having something fun for their kids to do. A district outside of Rochester, NY has high school kids run a carnival in the elementary gym the day of conferences. Parents are encouraged to drop their kids off in the gym before heading to their individual conference. Since individual conferences rarely take more than 20 minutes, parents are then encouraged to stay and participate in the carnival with their child. The carnival culminates with the principal sitting in a dunk tank. Each student gets one shot to put her under.

A fourth grade teacher we know in the Knoxville, TN public schools always has great tasting donut holes available on parent conference days. We know a high school that significantly increased participation at "meet and greet" nights by providing an inexpensive dinner of pizza and salad at the beginning of the event. Perhaps the best and least gimmicky way to attract parents is to have student-led conferences. Instead of the traditional conference where the teacher tells the parent(s) how the student is doing, the student leads the conference by explaining his own strengths and weaknesses. The student, with some teacher and parent input, plans goals and actions for continued progress, and usually shares a portfolio containing at least three items that represent his/her work. These can include tests and projects. The student can update everyone on community service requirements and invites parents and teacher(s) to attend. The best model of this we have seen is at Pittsfield Middle High School in Pittsfield, NH. Students in groups of 10-15 are assigned to a homeroom adviser who is a teacher, administrator or counselor. A shortened first period begins their day. The adviser's function is to monitor progress, provide support and connect with their students. Students remain in that group throughout the school year and as time for conferences near, the adviser leads them through the planning process. The adviser and student are present at each scheduled conference. The parent(s) and all of the student's teachers are invited. The student also can invite other influential adults in their lives. Since beginning student-led conferences, parent attendance reportedly went from 40-50% attendance to over 90% and has been sustained at that level since.

Do community outreach with students and invite specific parents to be involved. Community service is often a requirement for graduation. Involve your challenging parents in these efforts. One of the best ways to build cooperation is by working together towards a common purpose that is valued by all. Habitat for Humanity, Big Brothers Big Sisters, and Special Olympics are all organizations constantly seeking community volunteers. Encourage parents and their children to meet you at a local homeless shelter. Meeting on neutral ground with a specific task meant to help others is an amazing relationship-building tool for parents and kids. Difficult parents can become excellent partners in the planning and execution of such school wide initiatives. As the parent of an adolescent, it can be particularly difficult to find special moments to share. Good feelings develop when the school becomes a place where parents, students and teachers can share meaningful moments. We realize some of these ideas are time-consuming. View them as an investment in your relationship with that parent and their child.

Recognize holidays and birthdays. During the holiday season, send a card or e-card to the family along with a short personal greeting. Something simple such as:

> *To the Crawford family: Enjoy the holiday. Christina, I look forward to seeing you after break.*"

A birthday card from the teacher to a student with a personal message is a great way to acknowledge a special day and is greatly appreciated by most kids and parents.

Call or ask for occasional feedback. It is a good idea to seek parental input before you hear about problems. Be open to knowing how you are doing from the perspective of the parent. There may be parents that are harboring resentment about things that you are doing (or that they think you are doing), which may not be difficult to change. You might send a feedback survey a few times each year to either all or some of your parents so that you can stay informed. The following can be included:

> As a parent, you are so very important to your child's success at school. I am eager to know how you view your child's experience in my class. Please take a few moments to answer the following questions, since your feedback can be very helpful in making sure that your child is getting the best possible experience he/she can.
> 1. How do you think your child is doing in my class?
> 2. How do you think your child should be doing in my class?
> 3. What do you hear your child talking about that he/she likes?
> 4. Is there anything that can be improved that would make your child more successful? (Please be specific.)
> 5. Would you like to discuss any concerns you may have?
> 6. What is the best way and time to contact you?

Develop a method of feedback that works for you and parents.
When a parent is rarely satisfied and often questions your actions, develop a method of regular feedback that works for both of you. This can be a note, a phone call, or a chart that lets the parent know how the child is doing *(figure 3)*. Encourage parents to respond to your

SUCCESS FOR JOHNNY	
PUT FORTH EFFORT Comments:	Excellent 5 4 3 2 1 Poor
Your (parent) feedback or ideas to help me understand:	
DID HIS WORK WITH GOOD QUALITY Comments:	Excellent 5 4 3 2 1 Poor
Your feedback or ideas to help me understand:	
GOT ALONG WITH OTHERS Comments:	Excellent 5 4 3 2 1 Poor
Your feedback or ideas to help me understand:	
FOLLOWED THE RULES Comments:	Excellent 5 4 3 2 1 Poor
Your feedback or ideas to help me understand:	
HANDLED HIS EMOTIONS Comments:	Excellent 5 4 3 2 1 Poor

Figure 3

Invite difficult parents to spend time observing your class. As unpleasant as the thought might be to have a difficult parent observe, this can be a powerful tool towards inviting cooperation. It is particularly effective when parents are blaming you based upon what they heard from their child. When a child has been in trouble, it is common for them to tell their side of the story to their parent(s). Naturally no child says, *"Mrs. Jones got mad today because I was throwing flying missiles in the classroom, tapping my pencil endlessly and I constantly got out of my seat to bother other students."* Instead, most kids portray the teacher as having been unfair. When this happens regularly, invite parents to visit your class and then listen to strategies they might offer that can best help their child. Needless to say, it is best to initiate contact when problems are in their early stage and long before they have gained a major foothold.

Invite parents to share. One of the best ways to get parents positively involved in your classroom is to have them share personal interests and talents with your students. If you know or learn of a parent's special talent or interest, invite them to come in. You might even end a meeting about something else by inviting the parent to share. For example: *"I totally understand your concerns Ms. Huang, and I think you have some really great ideas. I'm glad we had a chance to meet. You know, I understand from Bobby that you are into tap dancing. I was wondering if you might come to class and show the children a few of the basics. I think this might be an especially worthwhile activity especially for some of my students who need a little more movement in their day. Would you be open to that?........When are you available?"*

Consult with other staff who know the family for suggestions. Chances are you are not the only one struggling with a challenging student. Touch base with a colleague or two who can provide insight and might be able to offer suggestions about how to most effectively communicate. For example, another teacher may know that Mrs. Santos is a very caring person with a harsh exterior that can feel intimidating. Since harshness often shuts down communication, having such knowledge helps the educator stay focused on the issue without becoming defensive. Don't be afraid to ask other teachers who had the student of concern what worked for them to improve the student's behavior or get better cooperation from the parent(s).

Chapter Eight
Strategies that PROVIDE SUPPORT & ADVICE for parents

Many difficult parents are struggling to guide and raise their challenging children in our complex world. This section offers tips to share with parents that can help with everyday practical challenges of parenting. Before giving advice, be sure to ask the parents if they want help. For example, "Mrs. Richard, I know you are struggling with Daniel as well. I would never tell you how to parents your son, but I would be more than willing to listen to your concerns and explore some ideas with you that might make things better. Is that something that would interest you?.... Would you like to think about it and let me know if you are interested?"

I once had a parent cry on my shoulder as she muttered, *"there is no manual that comes with getting pregnant and raising a child. I have no idea what to do with my son."* Dan was a senior and running the show at home. If mom said to come in for the night at eight, Dan would stroll in at eleven. She asked what to do. I suggested the importance of getting at why Dan was so defiant. Was he always like this? When did this behavior begin? Are there times that he is thoughtful and cooperative? She shared some information in response to my questions, which made me realize that the length and depth of the problem at home would likely require more intensive exploration. I also learned that he acts very responsibly at his after-school job with his boss having recently shared a glowing compliment about him with her. That gave me an opportunity to point out that it is often a much better sign of emotional health when a child acts out at home rather than in other places. We ended the conference by agreeing to have our school counselor contact her with referral information. Sometimes, the best support and advice we can offer is a caring, listening ear while acknowledging the need for intervention from an outside resource.

Understand what parents are up against. There are a fair number of children who can be quite gifted in whining their way to what they want. As noted in another section, informal surveys of teenagers found that most expect to ask for what they want nine times before getting it. The bottom line is today's youth are entirely prepared to endlessly persist in wearing their parents down in order to get what they want. This can include telling them what they want them to believe about incidents at school. Some parents feel guilty whenever they say "no" or when they challenge their child's view of an event. This can lead to an adversarial relationship between educator and parent, with some students more than happy to exploit it. When you have concerns you want to share with parents about their child or they have concerns about you, this can be a good time to show them that you understand what they are up against and assist them. For example,

"I find that it is not at all unusual for kids to complain when they don't get what they want or think they deserve. And some, like Melanie, are very persistent. They don't back down easily. At school, she can be strong about wanting things her way and gets pretty angry when things don't work out. I know she thinks she deserved a better grade and I'll be happy to tell you why I told her I didn't agree, but I wonder if she is as determined at home to have things her way as she can be at school? How do you handle this at home?"

This approach is likely to have parents open up about similar difficulties at home and gives you an opportunity to help reinforce the importance of learning an important life lesson and gives you a ton of credibility. For example: *"It sounds like when you hold firm she plays on your guilt and says, 'See, you don't really love me. I knew it.' When this does not work she gets angry and says, 'I hate you mom. You are so mean. I want to run away.' I know how difficult it can be to not give in at those times, but I also know that kids are seeking limits and while I've noticed that she gets grouchy when things don't go her way, I've also seen that she gets over it pretty quickly. Hold firm. Your expectations seem entirely reasonable, but she wants to take the easy way out."*

Help parents reward their children without buying things.
Many children expect to be tangibly rewarded for effort or achievement. They learn that an activity only has worth if there is a pay-off. Yet true success is accomplished through such values as hard work,

honesty, caring about others, and delaying gratification. Many parents appreciate learning or being reminded of ways that they can reinforce these values on a daily basis.

Kids feel really good when they are noticed for a thoughtful action that they did for others – it could be as simple as helping to carry in the groceries or as consuming as befriending a senior citizen. Remind parents at every opportunity to show excitement in their children's discoveries, acknowledge their insights in a conversation, notice an act of self-sacrifice, ask for an opinion and listen to their experiences and stories. Coordinate a volunteer day with Special Olympics and ask kids and their parents to help. Although such moments won't completely eliminate cravings for the hottest product in our extremely materialistic culture, they will help place a premium on the values that lead to real success and accomplishment.

WAYS OF REWARDING CHILDREN THAT COST NO MONEY

1. Show excitement in your child's discoveries
2. Acknowledge their insights in a conversation
3. Notice an act of self-sacrifice
4. Ask for their opinion
5. Listen to their experiences and stories

Teach parents how to give their children effective commands. Many parents who express anger at educators are actually quite frustrated at their own inability to get their children to comply at home. Problems at school are usually symptomatic of problems that parents have in gaining their child's compliance at home. With a small percentage of parents, it is impossible to get to a point in our relationship where they acknowledge problems at home. However, most parents are searching for answers, and if the teacher offers sufficient empathy and understanding, most parents become open to sharing their concerns. There are some effective tips we can offer when parents share frustrations around the problem of gaining compliance from their children at home. There are specific characteristics that can make commands effective.

They should be directly stated, specific and consist of one step.

They should be developmentally appropriate, phrased positively when possible, and presented one at a time. Approximately five-seconds between commands is minimum.

Verbal praise is offered after giving the command followed by a display of appreciation after compliance has been achieved.

A few examples follow:

"Joey, your room needs cleaning. Thank you so much for taking care of it."
After compliance:
"Wow Joey, I especially like the way you put your shoes away."

"Martha, we use our words when we are mad, not our fists. Thanks for using grown-up words like please and thank you."
After compliance:
"I am so proud at how well you used grown up words when Jeffrey interrupted your game without asking."

"Emily, I care too much to allow you to ride in Sally's car with a broken headlight. You can either allow me to drive you to the party, not go, or you can get another ride in a safe car."
After compliance:
"I appreciate your willingness to use good judgment last night by choosing a safe option."

Thank parents for their cooperation before getting it. Thanking a challenging person for doing what you ask before they do it dramatically increases the odds of the person complying. This is true for children and parents.
A few examples show how this approach works well when used by a teacher to either a parent or child:

47

To a parent: *"I can see that you are upset about what happened and you want to tell me what you think I should have done differently. Thanks for letting me know calmly and specifically.*

To a child: *"I know you didn't drop that piece of paper. Thanks so much for picking it up anyway. I appreciate it."*

When you want or need support from a parent that might be difficult to get. It can be very helpful to teach parents this method of gaining cooperation when they struggle to get compliance from their children. Try the following:

Identify exactly what you want parents to do to support your efforts in helping their child. *"It would be really helpful if you_____," or "I know Matt (child) and I can both count on you doing_____".*

Express your appreciation for the action *"Thanks so much for this important support that will help our child be successful".*

Evaluate the result *"I'll plan to call back tomorrow to let you know how it went. Thanks".*

Teach parents language that builds success. Teach parents how to encourage their children by giving them examples of things you say to motivate them. Then suggest that they try saying at least one of the comments every day for two weeks to each of your challenging students. At a parent conference and/or during an open school night let parents know how you try to encourage students and give them home-based examples like the ones below that they can use.

"You found a toy that Avi (your brother) likes after showing him some that he didn't like. ***Thank you for showing patience."***

*"****Your clothes were all over the floor and now they're hung up,*** *which probably makes it easier to find things."*

*"****I appreciate your focus*** *even though your homework looks challenging.*

You look ready to tackle it. Way to go."

"*You'd probably rather be doing something more fun, but right now **it looks like you're taking care of business.**"*

"**You're acting very grown-up** *(responsible) right now and it's really nice to see.*"

"**You hung in there** *and showed patience. Nice job.*"

"**I am really impressed** *with how you acted.*"

"**Your effort paid off.** *Congratulations.*"

"*Keep up the good work.*"

"**Your improvement is a joy** *to see. Keep it up.*"

"**I am one lucky parent to have a child** *who_____.*"

"*Wow,* **the progress I saw today** *when you did_____ is really neat.*"

"**You made my day** *when you_____.*"

"*That may not be the best grade, but you have lot to be proud of and I hope you are.*"

Show parents how to teach responsibility. Responsibility requires that individuals believe the things that happen to them are mostly a result of their own actions. You are late for an appointment because you decided to stop at a store to squeeze in one last errand and then had to wait in line unexpectedly long to pay your bill. Because you were late, you miss your appointment, and you have to reschedule for next week. Attributing lateness to your own poor planning (leaving your house later than you should) and the consequence to your own decision-making (trying to squeeze in another errand), you quickly learn not to make the same mistake again. However, if rescued from your mistake (earlier appointments are backed up and lateness has no consequence), you are more likely to repeat it. When individuals are responsible for what happens to them in any given situation, they develop an "internal locus of control." If you believe that forces outside your control cause things to happen, you have an "external locus of control." This results in excuse making. Responsibility means teaching children that actions have results / consequences. There are three skills associated with developing responsibility in kids – predicting, choosing and planning.

Predicting strategies.   In order to be responsible, children need to understand that certain behaviors bring predictable results. If children cannot connect what they do with what happens next, then no learning occurs. Predictability comes from consistency. If you say you will do something, do it. Keep your promises. Keep things on schedule. If you tell your chronically late awakening teenager that he will have to make his own plans to get to school if he misses the bus, follow through. Do not give him a ride. Teaching a forgetful child to bring materials to school is better accomplished by allowing her to experience the school consequences of being unprepared than running to school carrying the forgotten book bag. Show parents how to ask their children lots of predicting questions:

> *What do you think will happen if you don't get your assignment completed?*

> *What do you think your teacher would say if you gave her a compliment?*

> *How do you think your brother would react if you offered to share your favorite toy?*

> *What are some consequences that could happen if you keep picking on other kids?*

Choosing strategies. In order to learn responsibility, children must have more than one real choice. For example, telling a child to "say you're sorry or no TV," is a threat, not a choice, because no thought is required and no real options are presented. A choice is *"Saying you're sorry and/or doing something nice for a person you hurt are ways I know to make things right. Maybe there should also be no TV so you have time to think about what you did and how to make it better. What do you think will help you not make the same mistake again?"* When children are given real choices, there is no guarantee they will want any of them, but it is a beginning for learning how to be responsible. Give parents examples of how they can give real choices to teach responsibility:

> *"You can clean up your mess right now or you can do it in a half-hour."*

> *"When you are angry, you can tell how you feel or write a note."*

> *"You can eat what I cook or you can cook your dinner."*

> *"You can do the laundry or mow the lawn. It's up to you."*

> *"You can get your homework done before your favorite show or directly after."*

Planning strategies. The better we plan, the more likely we are to control what happens to us. Shopping lists, recipes, using navigation devices, directions and budgets are all ways of planning how to get what we want or where we go. A plan usually has a series of steps that need to be followed in order for a desired result to occur. Parents can teach this important skill by asking appropriate questions. For example: *"John, how can you earn enough money to buy that new video game you want?*

Help the child identify obstacles that might get in the way: *"Seems to me that if you work all those hours to earn enough, there may not be enough time to keep your grades up at school. When would homework and other responsibilities get done?"*

Help the child have a back-up: *"Can you think of some other ways to earn some money in case there isn't enough time to work and get everything else done?*

51

Finally, if a child's plan seems unworkable or would probably create other problems don't quit.

Keep on going: *"That solution won't work for me because* _____.
Let's think about one that could work for both of us. Do you have some other ideas?"

Show how to get beyond "I don't know." Some kids try to not engage in problem-solving by repeatedly saying "I don't know." They find that most adults eventually get frustrated and give-up. A solution that frequently works is to respectfully say, *"If you did know, what would you say?"*

Sometimes, persistence is needed to promote responsibility. Notice this example:

> Parent: *"So what are some things you might do to stay out of trouble?"*
>
> Child: *"I don't know."*
>
> Parent: *"Well, if you did know, what would you say?"*
>
> Child: *"I don't know."*
>
> Parent: *"It can be tough to come up with a solution, but if you had to guess, what would you say?"*
>
> Child: *"I said I don't know."*
>
> Parent: *"What are some things other kids do who don't get into trouble?"*

Encourage parents to talk with their children about classroom learning. Emphasize that most high-achieving students have parents who encourage them, talk with them about school, keep them focused on learning and homework, and help them plan for higher education. Whether they are discussing books, preparing for tests or projects, or helping with homework, parent involvement is a key factor in raising achievement. That said, it is common for virtually all students when asked by their parent(s) "how was school today," to give the predictable one-word answer: "good." To help facilitate parent communication with their children about classroom learning, prepare a suggestion sheet that parents can use.

Suggested questions to guide discussion are:

> *"What was one new idea you had or fact you learned today?"*

> *"Tell me two of the easiest assignments your teacher(s) gave you today."*

> *"What was most challenging about your class(es) today?"*

> *"When you were unsure about something at school today, what did you do?"*

> *"What happened next?"*

> *"What are some of the things from today's class that you think might be on the next test?"*

> *"Which part of your homework do you expect to do first?"*

> *"If your teacher could get you to be a little better at one thing, what do you think she would suggest?"*

Encourage parents to have meals with their children without distraction. Family dinners have become more the exception than the norm. Various surveys find that only one in three families eat together every day. Even more startling is that of those who eat together, the vast majority report having the television on in the background. As well, it has become commonplace to see families out to dinner with everyone looking at their cell phones rather than interacting with each other. The success of our students largely depends upon parental involvement and interest in their education. The reality is that all people have to eat and it can be during this time that focused, distraction free discussion time should be emphasized. A sit down meal can be a wonderful opportunity for children to learn social skills, conversational skills and table manners. Be respectful of differences among families while suggesting gradual increases in distraction free family meals. Suggest that parents use this time to learn more about what is happening in their children's lives. Share some conversation starters with them. *For example*:

> *"What is the funniest thing that happened today?"*

> *"What was the most enjoyable thing you did today?"*

> *"What was the most boring thing you had to do today?"*

> *"What was your free time (recess) like? Did you have any? What did you do?"*

> *"When someone makes a mistake, how is that usually handled by your teacher?"*

> *"What was the yuckiest lunch you saw someone eat today?"*

> *"What is something you did or accomplished that you wish had been noticed?"*

> *"Did you hear any words that could have been said more politely to someone?"*

> *"Tell me one new thing you learned today?"*

> *"If you had to trade places with someone else today, who would it have been? Why?"*

Chapter Nine

Strategies for HANDLING DIFFICULT MOMENTS *with parents*

This section provides strategies to use when parents complain, blame, criticize or go over your head. In addition, specific methods are suggested to gain cooperation from difficult parents when students are misbehaving. Numerous strategies that show how to defuse angry parents are offered. Finally, practical ways are described to gain administrative support while working with difficult parents and their children.

Put yourself in their shoes. Before talking to a parent, put yourself at the receiving end of what you are about to share. How would you want the teacher to talk to you? What would you want to hear about your child? How might you react if it was all negative? Would you appreciate hearing something positive? How would you feel towards the teacher if s/he asked you questions that could help him/her learn more about your child's strengths and needs? Most difficult parents are better able to handle criticism when they believe you truly care about their child and that you recognize his strengths as well as behaviors that need improvement. A good rule to remember is that criticism is only criticism when it is directly accompanied by compliment.

Stay firm when values are challenged. When parents challenge or accuse, stay focused on the values you are supporting. Nothing undermines classroom discipline more than backing down on what is educationally sound in the name of doing what is "politically correct." I recall a case involving the temporary suspension of a coach who held a few sports practices at the school bus garage, having his players cleaning buses after an incident in which some of the team made a mess of the bus while in route to a game. The suspension of the coach followed complaints of group punishment by a few parents. Clearly, the coach was upholding the value that a team is accountable for all its members. His choice to have them clean buses was also a natural outcome of the behavior. He should have been praised for this thoughtful action rather than put through such stress.

Strategize with administration and/or special area educators when a parent complains. It is certainly difficult to anticipate all of the factors that may lead to parental dissatisfaction. However, when a parent initiates a complaint directly to you and you feel unable to resolve the complaint in a manner that seems satisfactory to the parent, inform your administrator and/or a trusted colleague right away. Tell the administrator what happened and the specifics that led to parental dissatisfaction. Explain that despite your direct efforts, you were unable to feel that the matter was satisfactorily resolved and why. It is then wise to brainstorm possible next steps with the administrator. You might suggest that the administrator call to explain his knowledge of the situation along with your concern about it while exploring what might be done. You could ask the administrator to make herself available for a three-way conference in a mediator role that might lead to a resolution of the issue. You might just simply ask the administrator for advice on how to best proceed from here. Try not to wait for the parent to contact the administrator. When you have disagreed with a parent while believing that you are upholding a position that is in the best educational interest of the student, initiate contact with your administrator and express your perspective in a confident, proactive manner while keeping open to a possible way of solving the problem that you hadn't considered.

Actively listen to all complaints. The most important skill to develop in order to defuse angry people is the ability to listen to others and then let them know that you captured the essence of both their content and their feelings. Successful job candidates often do more listening than talking during an interview. The first step is to put away what you want to say and really hear what somebody else is trying to tell you. This is not easy! Parents will hear your concerns much more clearly and less defensively when they feel that you truly understand their perspective. It is important to learn and practice the art of paraphrasing. After you hear somebody express a thought or feeling, try paraphrasing what was just said. Examples are as follows:

"What you are saying is..."

"If I understand, I believe you meant (feeling)..."

"You seem to be thinking (feeling)..."

"If I hear you correctly, you are telling me that..."

"How (exciting, frustrating, annoying) it must be when..."

Being a great listener means going beyond the content. Try giving feedback that gets at the parent's feelings:
"It must be difficult when Billy comes home unhappy."

"Sounds like you are in a tough spot. On the one hand you love your child and want to be supportive, but on the other hand you're upset to be hearing about some of the poor decisions she's been making."

"Oh my gosh, you must feel..."

"It comes across like you are feeling..."

When you are at a loss and the words just aren't flowing, keep communication going with the parent. Use simple words like wow, really, and I see, accompanied by caring body language conveyed with eye contact and a friendly look. Nod your head up and down and smile. Even when annoyed, smile!

Communicate your thoughts clearly. Openly sharing our wants and needs sets the stage to engage in joint problem-solving so that decisions are more often based on cooperation between educators and parents. The language, body language and tone we use can be the difference between alienating a parent or eliciting cooperation. Examples of "opening" language we can use to communicate our thoughts clearly and gain cooperation from parents follow:

"I believe what will help (student's name) be most successful is_____."

"From my point of view, it is especially important to _____.

"I am open to ideas that will help (student's name) learn to be even more independent. Do you have any suggestions?"

"I am excited to see that when we do_____, (student's name) experiences more success."

"I'm not sure of the best solution, but what makes most sense to me is_____.

"It is my hope that we can work closely together to make sure (student's name) has a great year."

All of these "openers" can be followed with, *"What are your thoughts about that?"* If for some reason a parent is angry, focus on staying calm and keeping your voice controlled. Remain cordial and friendly even when a parent is being disagreeable. Nod to show you hear them and make good eye contact when they are talking to you.

Set limits when necessary, but stay open to other ways. Keep being guided by your main goals: helping students be successful and teaching them important life lessons about responsibility. When students break rules that require a meeting with parents, stay focused on these goals, but keep an open mind to parental suggestions that could achieve the same goals with more student or parent support.

For example,

"If I understand your concerns correctly, you think it is very important for Samantha to be active during recess so that she can better concentrate when she is in her seat. I'm all for that. My view about keeping Samantha in the classroom during recess is to give her some extra time to get her work done. Let's see if we can think of some other ways that might give her the activity she needs while making sure that her work gets done. I'm thinking she could do it at home under your supervision,

work in class with another student or continue to do it during recess and have more activity at home. How do these ideas sound? How do you see it?"

After some possible solutions are discussed you might conclude,

"I think we ought to share these thoughts with Samantha. She might even have some ideas we haven't thought of. Do you want to join me or would you prefer that I just meet with her?"

Stay personally connected to parents without taking what they do and say personally. Many educators acknowledge how much they struggle keeping their anger in check when a parent says or does offensive things. While it is natural to impulsively react when our buttons are pushed, being a professional means stopping and thinking before acting (exactly as we teach students who struggle with self-control). Try hard to stay personally connected without taking personally what they do and say. Stay focused on what you want. Ask yourself if an emotional reaction to this parent gets you closer to what you want. Try to see the parent as a "misguided advocate" or an emotionally fragile person. Strange as it may sound, look at the attack as an opportunity for you to strengthen your 'mental toughness' or 'grit.' Take a few deep breaths or a quick bathroom break to compose yourself. Remember that an angry parent is advocating for her child and while you aren't a punching bag for the parent's frustration and will not accept disrespectful treatment, staying calm is always the best option. Once you defuse yourself, you will remain in charge during the conference, which enables you to put yourself in their shoes, think clearly and act with purpose rather than emotion.

Give parents the first chance to intervene. Give parents a chance to influence their children before sending students to the office or counselor for a disciplinary intervention. Let parent(s) know that there recently have been some difficulties caused by their child's behavior that are getting beyond your control. Call home or invite parents in for a conference.

Start your conversation by thanking them. Thank them for coming or giving you the time to discuss their child. *"Thanks for coming in*

today. I know you are very busy and I appreciate you taking a few minutes for this very important matter."

Begin with something positive. *"I want to start by saying how pleased I have been with Glen's work habits. He has been prepared with his work and often participates in class."*

Proceed by identifying the current problem. *"Glen has been having some trouble these last few days using proper language and when I remind him, he has been getting angry and argumentative."*

Let parents know that they are a possible alternative to a corrective plan and request their assistance. *"I've been thinking about writing referrals for disciplinary action and asking his counselor to meet with him, but I first wanted to ask for your assistance."*

Be specific about the kind of assistance you want. *"Can I count on getting your help in discussing this with him and making sure he remembers to use proper language?"* If a willingness to cooperate is expressed:

Conclude by thanking the parent and setting a time for follow-up. *"I appreciate your help on this. After you talk to him, I would especially like to know how I might be able to help. Please call me by Thursday and let me know how your conversation went."*

Try to defuse angry parents quickly. One of the quickest ways to defuse when verbally attacked is to agree with whatever is said. There may be some truth to the accusation, but even if there is none, nothing is gained by arguing. Remember, the goal is to have an unhappy parent leave the conference being more supportive of what you are doing or going to do to help their child be more successful. For example, Pete's father, Mr. Greco initiates contact with his teacher or responds to a request for a conference by blaming. He says, *"Pete tells me that he is very bored in your class. What are you going to do to be more interesting?"* With the goal to defuse, a good response is, *"There is probably some truth to what he says. In fact, it is always my goal to be more interesting, and I will do my best* *to make my lessons even better."* It is best to conclude with, *"Bored or not, I'm sure you agree that we need to help Pete find better ways than humming and making other noises when he is bored."* Offer examples of more appropriate ways to express boredom and/or ask the parent what s/he thinks a worker should do to remain productive at work.

One of the best ways to defuse an angry parent is to acknowledge their anger as a message of support for their child. We can respect their support if not their means of expression. The following procedures can be very effective in defusing an angry parent.

Acknowledge their perspective and ask for feedback. *"Wow, Mrs. Brown, I had no idea how angry you would be. If I understand things correctly, you are particularly upset about the consequences Livan received for fighting. Am I right about that?"*

Agree that there may be other ways to solve the problem. *"Rarely is there only one way to solve a problem. This is what I thought be best for your child, but if you have other ideas that can make things better, please share your thoughts before you leave."*

Set limits when your boundaries are crossed. *"Please know that while I want to hear your ideas, it is not okay that you raise your voice and use inappropriate language. I don't talk to parents or students in that way and I appreciate being spoken to respectfully as well. Now what do you want to tell me?"*

Be honest about what you can do and what you can't. *"I think it is very important that no matter how upset Livan gets, we all let him know that at school it is never okay to fight to solve problems. School is a place for learning and neither Livan nor any of my other students are going to be able to learn if they are thinking about, planning or actually fighting. Please do not ask that I excuse his behavior even if somebody else started it."*

Remind the parent that you are always guided by success and responsibility, not by comparing students. If parents ever want to compare your actions toward their child with another, refuse to make these comparisons. *"Mrs. Brown, I am not at liberty to tell you why I might have used a different consequence with another child. I consider that to be a private* matter between myself, that child and his family. My goal is to always help each of my students become more successful and learn more about responsibility. I decided that this was the best thing to do for your child. But I'm certainly far from perfect and there may well be a better way in the future. Perhaps you can help me understand what is most helpful to support your child in becoming more successful. If you have thoughts about how your child might learn better from a different consequence, I am happy to listen."

Offer a third party if there is a stalemate or if the parent is excessively offensive. "I don't think we are going to be able to agree on this." OR "I will not be spoken to in this way. I think Mrs. Donovan is a good choice to help us. Do you want to arrange an appointment or should I?"

Ask the student to leave if the parent is inappropriate in the student's presence. It is often beneficial for a student to be present during a parent conference concerning his behavior. However, sometimes parents may become too upset to use appropriate manners by acting in verbally or otherwise abusive ways. Should that occur, the educator needs to take charge and protect the student by asking the student to leave. Say to the student something like,
"Carlos, I need to have a private word with your parents. Please step outside." Then deal directly with parents in one or more ways already suggested. With a very young child, try to arrange a specific place. Say to all present, "I think it is best if just the grown-ups keep talking right now, so I am going to call Mrs. Smith (fellow teacher that can be easily reached) and see if Carlos can stay with her for a few minutes while we talk." If there are no alternatives available, it is probably best to end the conference and try again at another time.

Apologize after being accused even when you feel you did nothing wrong. Sincere apologies to parents and students convey honesty and define us as imperfect, thoughtful and approachable. **For example,**
"Charkendra, I lost my patience with you earlier and I am sorry about some of the things I said. That wasn't right of me. I realize calling you out in front of your friends makes you upset. But I am impulsive sometimes just like you. In fact, you and I are similar in that way. Is there anything you think you can do differently next time?"

In fact, teachers who communicate openly with their students rarely have problems with parents, but the same strategy can be used with an accusatory parent. ***For example***, *"In no way was it my intention for Sabrina to think that I was blaming her, and if that's what she came away with from our conference, I want to apologize to you and her. I guess I'll need to find a better way to give feedback."*

  If this gets you nowhere, do not continue trying to change their mind. Since you are unlikely to convince the parent of your perspective, act as if you made a mistake and offer to work harder. For example, *"Mr. Lopez, I am very sorry that you and Rodrigo (your son) feel as strongly as you do. It is not my desire to lose him as a student or lose your support as a parent. I will work harder to gain your trust in the future. Thanks for letting me know some of the things you would like to see me do."* Apologizing takes a lot less time than trying to explain facts or circumstances to somebody whose primary interest is conflict.

Conclusion

It is our sincere hope that the many strategies offered throughout this book have provided and will continue to provide fellow educators with practical ways of handling tough parents, difficult kids, and difficult situations. Many methods have been offered to positively influence the behavior and cooperation of belligerent or uninvolved parents. However, there are times when all the right moves still do not produce the best results. My friend and now retired teacher Howard Itkin, told of a parent whose complaints about her daughter's experience in his second grade class led to a time-consuming conference and the development of a plan that seemed to meet with everyone's approval. Howard remembered feeling very pleased and enthusiastic. The next day, the parent withdrew her daughter from the school.

Fortunately, most parents care for their children, and want what is best for them. The vast majority are reasonable in their dealings with others. While most parents love their children and want only the best, many do not have a real understanding of how much commitment at home is needed for their children to be successful in school. On a recent visit with 10 year-old Victor, our "little" in the Big Brothers Big Sisters program, he spontaneously said he would never want to go to college because he wouldn't want to leave his family. When I asked this very bright boy if he knew anyone in his neighborhood who was going to college, Victor could not think of a single person. Sadly, Victor is one of many who face an uphill struggle to success because he has no community context for how education can really improve life. From an early age, most students whose parents are successful understand that doing well in school is important and highly valued. Well intentioned parents race to live in neighborhoods with the "best" schools, somehow believing that it is really the school that makes all the difference. The primary responsibility for a child's success or failure is placed on the school rather than on harder to face issues such as effort and work ethic, family dynamics and sense of entitlement. Too willing are some parents to place blame for low achievement and poor behavior on everybody other than themselves and their child. Within these realities it is understandable that frustration and even disgust can set in. Yet to be and remain a truly effective educator we must rise beyond the natural tendency to become disenchanted and angry when we are directly affected. We must continuously view what we do as special and important because it is. We must listen and consider but not take personally unwarranted attacks. We must do our best to help students achieve success and therefore hope for a good life, especially when family and community fail to do its fair share.

Finally, we need to do what this book is about: help parents to become our strong partners even when they avoid or provoke us, so that together we can help guide their children to become successful, responsible adults.

Reference & Bibliography

Canfield, J., Hansen, M. V., McPherson, J. (2004). *Chicken Soup for the Soul Cartoons for Teachers*, Deerfield Beach, FL: Health Communications Inc.

Curwin, R. L., Mendler, A. N., Mendler, B. D. (2008). *Discipline with Dignity (rev. ed.)* Alexandria, VA: Association for Supervision and Curriculum Development.

Gladwell, M. (2005) *Blink*. New York: Little Brown & Co.

Levinson, W. (1997) "Physician-Patient Communication: The Relationship with Malpractice Claims Among Primary Care Physicians and Surgeons." *Journal of the American Medical Association* 277, no. 7.

Mendler, A. N. (2007). *More What Do I Do When...........*Bloomington, IN: Solution Tree.

Mendler, A. N. (2001). *Connecting with Students*. Alexandria, VA: Association of Supervision and Curriculum Development.

Mendler, A. N. (2000). *Motivating Students Who Don't Care*. Blooming, IN: Solution Tree.

Mendler, A. N., (2012). *Power Struggles, Successful techniques for educators*. Bloomington, IN: Solution Tree.

Mendler, A.N. (2012). *When Teaching Gets Tough*. Alexandria, VA: Association for Supervision and Curriculum Development

Mendler, A. N. (2014). *The Resilient Teacher*. Alexandria, VA: Association for Supervision and Curriculum Development.

Mendler, B. D., Curwin, R.L., Mendler, A. N. (2008). *Strategies for Successful Classroom Management*. Thousand Oaks, CA: Corwin Press